Education in Movement
in the Infant School

Education in Movement
in the Infant School

W. McD. CAMERON
Tutor-in-charge, Harold Court College,
Brentwood College of Education

MARJORIE CAMERON
Deputy Head, Westlands Infant School,
Chelmsford

BASIL BLACKWELL · OXFORD

© Basil Blackwell 1969
Reprinted 1971
0 631 95340 X

Filmset by Photoprint Plates Ltd., Wickford

Printed in Great Britain by
Wm. Clowes & Sons Ltd., London and Beccles

Bound by Kemp Hall Bindery, Oxford

CONTENTS

Foreword

MISS PEGGY PLEASANCE
Principal Lecturer, Head of Department of Physical Education,
Brentwood College of Education.

This practical textbook has been written in response to many requests from Infants teachers who feel the need for guidance in the teaching of Movement Education. The authors aim to help teachers apply Rudolf Laban's principles of movement to the teaching of Infant Movement Education, giving practical advice with regard to planning, organising and teaching of the various aspects of Movement Education. For the inexperienced teacher, detailed help is given in the form of lessons together with suggested tasks. These suggestions are a result of many years experience in working practically with children of this age.

The authors are convinced that teaching cannot be learnt from a book, and it is their earnest hope that the teacher who reads this book will eventually develop sufficient confidence and understanding to assess the needs of the children in her class, devising her own tasks and bringing her own individual approach to the work.

I am certain that those who are seeking understanding, help and guidance in the presentation of Movement Education in the Infants School will find this book of considerable help.

P. A. Pleasance.

Brentwood,
May, 1968.

'A school is not merely a teaching shop it must transmit values and attitudes. It is a community in which children learn to live first and foremost as children and not future adults. In family life children learn to live with people of all ages. The school sets out deliberately to devise the right environment for children, to allow them to be themselves and to develop in the way and at the pace appropriate to them. It tries to equalise opportunities and to compensate for handicaps. It lays special stress on individual discovery, on first hand experience and on opportunities for creative work. It insists that knowledge does not fall into neatly separate compartments and that work and play are not opposite but complementary. A child brought up in such an atmosphere at all stages of his education has some hope of becoming a balanced and mature adult and of being able to live in, to contribute to, and to look critically at the society of which he forms a part. Not all primary schools correspond to this picture, but it does represent a general and quickening trend.'

'Children and their Primary Schools':
Central Advisory Council for Education (England)
Vol: I, para: 505

Introduction

It is only by observation and the sharing of ideas, whether through discussion or the written word, that the philosophy and practice of education can efficiently develop. Only after experiment and assessment, success and development, or failure and rejection can our individual ideas be proved valid and be crystallised. Being able to share something of the work of others leads to a widening of our own ideas, fresh stimulation and an awareness of new factors of assessment.

Few books on work in Physical Education in the Infant School have been written in recent years. 'Movement Education for Infants' published by the Inner London Education Authority has been a notable contribution. Teachers, both in schools and colleges of education, have been aware of its impact. Its authors had perceived that teachers and students require a knowledge of teaching technique based on sound educational judgement. To be effective teachers they must be able not only to assess the needs of the children in terms of their physical, social and emotional development but also be continuously re-assessing the efficacy of their lessons.

The demand we place on our teachers in infant schools is high. Not content with expecting them to be psychologists, philosophers and practitioners of a wide range of skills, we expect their class-rooms to be colourful and stimulating and their lessons full of creative opportunities for the children.

Knowledge in itself is not enough. It is only by teaching and handling the material of the lesson in the classroom situation that we, as teachers, can grow and develop.

This book is a signpost to indicate the way and not a vehicle to carry the teacher. Its object is not to list material for the teacher to use, but to show how the teacher can prepare lessons suitable to the needs of her class. Its aim is the development of understanding and expertise. It is not a reference book which requires no thought on the part of the teacher. It is hoped that through it teachers will be enabled to present a balanced programme, related to the child's world, having regard to the stage of development of the children in their classes.

The teacher should try to guide the children through experience to understanding and skill, and not try to impose upon them adult concepts of movement and relationships. Through our movement education lessons we hope to embark on a search for skills: skills of fluency and efficiency, in using the body as a tool and as a means of expression; skills in relationships and in working with consideration for others. The function of this book is to show how lessons and situations may be devised where such skills may be explored and developed.

The Infant School is not to be thought of merely as a preparatory stage for the Junior School. It represents a stage in its own right and our teaching should stimulate and nurture the child's growth in all its aspects.

There are some who will question the decision to call the major aspects of the programme Gymnastics, Dance and Games. It was decided to retain these terms of common experience for the sake of clarity and understanding.

Throughout the book the feminine pronoun will be used to refer to the teacher and the masculine pronoun to refer to the child.

Particular mention must be made of our colleague and very great friend Peggy Pleasance for her help and advice throughout the planning and writing of the book. Without her encouragement it would never have reached completion.

We must also thank Mrs. J. Briggs and Dr. S. Bridges of Brentwood College of Education for reading the script; Mrs. M. Ball who took the photographs and the Head-teachers of Mead Infants School, Havering; Stanford-le-Hope Infants School, Essex; and Upton County Primary School, Bexley for allowing us to record the children of their schools at work. To Mrs. J. Britton for her patience both in typing the manuscript, and with us, we must record an especial debt of gratitude.

This book represents a stage in development; comments, suggestions and constructive criticism will, therefore, be most welcome.

Marjorie Cameron

Chelmsford,   W. McD. Cameron

   April, 1968.

CHAPTER ONE
Education in the Infant School

Education may be defined as the result of exposure to situations which modify the development of the individual. This exposure may be controlled for the positive development of that person and in such a way as to contribute to the welfare of society. Teachers are concerned with what A. E. Peel calls the 'designed aspect' of Education, the aim of which is 'to promote the development of a well integrated person capable of exercising such responsibility in society as his powers allow'.[1] As the child grows his needs will change; so, too, will his response to adults. Contact, to be effective, must be accordingly modified. The younger the child the more susceptible he is to external influences. He has little background or acquired behaviour to modify the effects of new experience. That the early period of life is called the formative years is no empty cliché. The nursery and infant stages are the most important and significant of the child's school life. It is vital that during these years is laid the foundation for his full development of confidence and independence. Only through the recognition of individual achievement and consequent satisfaction come assurance and adjustment within the group.

The infant school, it is maintained, has a two fold function – to cater for the present needs of the child and to prepare him for his future life. It cannot, however, be stressed sufficiently that the best insurance for fulfilling the second aim is to ensure that our approach to education is appropriate to the child. It is, perhaps, pertinent to remember John Dewey's words 'Education is a process of living and not a preparation for future living'. The significance of the first part of the text 'When I was a child I spoke like a child, I thought like a child, I reasoned like a child; when I became a man I gave up childish ways'[2] is so often overlooked.

A child has the right to be treated at the stage at which he is,

[1] A. E. Peel, *The Psychological Basis of Education* (1956), Oliver and Boyd, p. 4.
[2] St. Paul: First Epistle to the Corinthians, ch: 13, v. 11

1

and not hurried towards a preconceived adult pattern of his future development. It is too often the case that a child is forced, exposed, manipulated and his growth subjected to such inappropriate conditions that only his natural resilience enables him to survive. In order to be effective the whole atmosphere, environment and opportunities offered must be appropriate to him and his rate of learning.

We have already referred to the time spent at this stage as the formative years, so the query 'formed for what?' also demands careful consideration. The essential culture, social attitudes, standards, criteria and skills required vary from one generation to the next. The child's adjustment and absorption (not submersion) in the society of which he will eventually be a part requires our consideration. How we achieve the dual function of preserving his individuality and at the same time of preparing him to contribute to the society of the future in which he will find himself is a problem to exercise all thinking educationalists. Society itself is evolving, shifting its emphases and challenging many of its established concepts. This makes the task of the progressive teacher even more critical. As the nature of society changes so its demands vary and its educative processes are modified. Flexible, resilient adults ready to adjust themselves to circumstance, who are forward-looking, progressive and considerate will be necessary if a full, happy and rich future is to be ensured.

In the Infant School the approach to this problem has been largely resolved. Creative activities have been happily integrated with skill learning. The concurrent presentation of opportunities to develop skills in physical activity, in reading, in number and in the manipulation of a wide variety of materials while ensuring social integration and the flowering of individual personality has served to emphasise the understanding and progressive nature of the infants' teacher. The education to which the children are exposed is soundly based on what is known of their psychological, physical and social aptitudes and needs. Through participation in the learning process, through activity and individual attention comes the happy atmosphere characteristic of our most efficient schools. Children are free and not confined. They are enabled to learn in a variety of ways through experience and interest at a pace suitable to each individual. Time-tables, and even activities within a single lesson, are flexible. The colourful, stimulating, varied environment of the classroom is a constant encouragement to the child's imagination. Teachers by their approachability, response and concern for the things which interest children are, however, the greatest factor. The maximum contribution to the child's growth, in all its aspects, can be made only in the permissive atmosphere of the modern infant school. Through the individual sense of achievement given in such a school grow an interest and a desire to work with others. Perhaps with a partner, perhaps as a member of what may be at first an unstable group come a readiness to listen and a willingness to subjugate personal inclination. Through co-operation, individuality is not lost; the child becomes less self-centred and contributes to the common effort for the common good.

The younger the child, the greater is his need for freedom and movement. Play is not a waste of time but the most valuable use to which time can be put. The adjustment to living in later life depends largely on the quality, quantity and type of play allowed to the child.

The Infant School should give a child opportunity for the identification of himself and the discovery of his part as an individual in the community. His adjustment and socialisation are part of his growth and development. Social skills require at least as great an emphasis as the manipulative skills of body and mind. The social skills within the child's peer group are often neglected in trying to force an artificial adjustment to the adult world. A child needs constant assurance, encouragement and opportunity for independent action. The individual approach to teaching has made possible the development of vertical grouping in schools and the contribution of this form of organisation has been recognised.

In education today much is heard of creativity—a word often misapplied and certainly over-used. It has been held capable of many and varied interpretations. If we state that in this book we take it to mean the individual contribution of a child to which something personal has been given, in either form or method of application, much argument may be saved. Creativity may vary in its scope, level and degree. It may appear under many different guises but it has its part to play in all aspects of the curriculum. Confidence is related to the child's ability to contribute something —part of which is original. In doing this he reveals something of

3

himself. As security is vital, both the child and his product need care in handling. He needs encouragement, his eagerness must not be blunted. No child should ever be made to feel failure or be unfavourably compared to his fellows. But children do not learn efficiently in the light of nature purely by trial and error. For efficient learning and optimum development the help, stimulation and guidance of a teacher are constantly required. The border between these and interference must not be violated.

The general approach to activity in the Infant School is an exploratory one through a variety of media. From experience and perception the child is led to understanding and to the application of his knowledge in a different situation. Exploration was his first method of learning and in the early months of life was mainly physical in character.

To develop responsibility a child must be given responsibility but, as with all other aspects of our approach, only to that degree which he can manage. The natural, spontaneous urges of the child need to be channelled so that he develops perception with sensitivity. It may be felt that learning situations need to be contrived and created by the teacher, but with experience it will be seen that opportunities for these abound and are immediately available at all times. Our approach to the teaching of the infant child is not to be thought of as merely 'doing' because it is based on activity and participation. It is learning through experience at first hand.

Physical education is that aspect of education concerned with educating the body/mind through movement—movement using the body as a means of expression and communication, movement using the body for the manipulation of external objects and movement to perform purposive tasks of body management. These are functional movements concerned with specific purpose and other forms of movement concerned with communication of ideas or mood. Gymnastics and games are functional, concerned with the management of the body in tackling a challenge posed by the environment or by the nature of the equipment. Dance uses the body more creatively and is concerned with feeling.

For experiment to be purposeful the field of investigation must be in part based on previous knowledge and experience. The area of investigation needs to be defined if the investigation is to be in depth. Understanding of the possibilities of movement and some criteria of assessment are essential.

4

In the field of movement education all these have been made possible because of the analysis of movement made by Rudolph Laban. Briefly, his analysis tells us how we may move, where we may move and in what ways we may move our bodies. To create situations which will stimulate the child to improve his powers and abilities and at the same time develop an awareness of the possibilities of movement the teacher must have a knowledge of Laban's analysis. The teacher must be able to observe accurately and to assess the work in terms of quality[1] and suitability so that he can aid subsequent development by advice and suggestion. The quality of education at this stage is directly related to the teacher's understanding of the child and her ability to relate this to modern methods in education.

The Infant School by its emphasis on the development of the child's potential at a rate appropriate to him, on the interest of the world about us, and on awakening the awareness of others, should lay what Professor Ben Morris calls the foundations of the arts of civilised life. These he defined in his paper given at Nottingham in July, 1966, as:

1 Love, sympathy and respect for others.
2 Enjoyment of the world, of beauty, of shared experience, of the mystery of an unfathomable universe.
3 Co-operation.
4 Aspirations towards personal and community achievement in the whole range of civilised activities.
5 Responsibility for one's own actions with which goes a real measure of independence of mind and heart.[2]

1 The term quality refers to a high standard of work. In place of the word 'qualities', previously used in Laban's analysis of movement, the word 'elements' will be used in this book.
2 The New Curriculum (H.M.S.O.) p. 7. lines 3–10.

CHAPTER TWO

Analysis of Movement

Movement may be considered under three main headings:
(1) Ways in which we may use our bodies;
(2) How we move, analysed in terms of Time, Weight and the qualitative element of Space;
(3) Where we move, which focuses attention on the way in which we use space.

(1) THE BODY IN ACTION

Our bodies are able to bend, stretch and twist. Since the body is flexible and its parts can also act independently, the shapes it can assume are very varied; they may be classified as twisted, curled, stretched, long, wide, symmetrical or asymmetrical. Shape is not to be thought of merely as something static but as a result of constantly changing body action. Curling, stretching and twisting are much more dynamic and appropriate than showing a curled, stretched or twisted position.

The body's weight may be taken on many individual, and combinations of, different parts of the body. The degree of skill needed to balance on these or to transfer weight between them varies according to the size of the base, the distribution of the weight and the height of the centre of gravity. To transfer weight smoothly and logically in a variety of ways often demands a high degree of skill and strength. Weight may be transferred to adjacent parts of the body continuously as in rolling, or to non-adjacent parts of the body which results in a step-like action.

Parts of the body may also be used to either initiate or lead a movement. Expressive movement can be developed by the child while his body is travelling, turning, advancing, retreating, rising, sinking, opening or closing.

From being conscious of how he is using his body in different situations and from perceptive teaching, the child comes to acquire a vocabulary of movement. From a consciousness of his body in

6

action he arrives at a knowledge of the variety of ways in which his body can move. He also develops a feeling for and an awareness of economical and effective movement.

Moving into stretching

(2)   THE ELEMENTS OF MOVEMENT

(a)   Time element. Laban in his analysis considered the time in which movement took place. To the extremes he gave the term 'sudden' and 'sustained'. The first was used to refer to movement which took place over a very short period of time and 'sustained' to indicate movement maintained over a long period. Sustained movement entails indulging in the use of time. This conception is difficult for children. At the infant stage it may be better for children to think in the more concrete terms of speed which represents the qualitative use of time. We call the two extremes simply quick and slow. Within these two limits fall a whole variety of speeds, accelerations, decelerations, combinations and rhythms.

(b)   Weight element. Our bodies are subject to the force of gravity. This we fight when we move, and fight more strongly when we jump. We give in to or yield to the force of gravity when our body or its parts are lowered or sink. In all situations the power required to move our bodies or external objects obviously varies and we may use our strength delicately or more strongly. Laban called these two extremes 'fine' and 'firm' touch. With children we tend to use the word 'strong' in place of firm touch and a variety of words such as 'gentle', 'soft' and 'light' in place of fine touch. Teachers need to be able to distinguish between strong and heavy movements.

(c)   Space element. Movement may be analysed qualitatively in terms of space, whether it is flexible or direct in its application. To indulge in space is to take a roundabout path whereas to use space with the greatest economy is to take a direct route. At the infant stage, the words 'straight' and 'twisted' are more easily understood.

(3)   SPACE ASPECT

The use of space can be considered in two contexts: first, the space immediate to the body, known as personal space. This is a roughly spherical shape in which are contained all the possible movements and extensions of the body from its centre or a fixed base. Secondly, the space of the hall or environment in which we can travel, including any apparatus which we may negotiate. This is known as general space. Spatial movement may be analysed in terms of:

(a)   Direction—forwards, backwards, sideways, upwards, downwards, diagonally and in combinations of these.

(b)   Level—near the floor, high in the air and in the space between. For convenience we divide movements into those of deep, medium and high level.

(c)   Pathway—this is concerned with the use of space on the floor, on apparatus or by a body part in the air where the pathway of the movement may be traced. This may be of a straight, angular, curved or twisting nature.

(d)   Relationship to the body centre—movement may start near the body and move directly away or it may move in the reverse direction. Alternatively, the movement may travel round the body centre.

Remembering this analysis of the use of space will contribute much to the lesson. It is important to know not only how space can be used but also how the body can best adapt itself to movement within its space. We should ensure balance and control in the different uses of space and develop in particular the children's ability to work independently without interfering with one another.

FLOW

This is concerned with the transition of the body from one position to another. A movement sequence may be smooth, showing control, logical development and balance, or it may be unco-ordinated and lacking in ease.

The term 'bound flow' is used for a movement that can be stopped easily at any point. This is in contrast to 'free flow' which is used to describe a movement which is not easily stopped and which should continue to its logical conclusion. The ability of the child to link smoothly the different parts of an activity is an aspect of skilled movement which is one of our objectives.

EFFORT

Although the basic Effort Actions analysed by Laban will not be used directly as part of the armoury of teaching, an understanding of the Effort Actions will aid the clarity of the teacher's perception. The three motion factors of Time, Weight and Space have as their limits sudden and sustained, firm and fine touch and direct and flexible movement. Since all three factors are present in any movement the teacher should be able, after practice, to perceive them in action. When they are combined, the eight effort sections listed below result.

Effort Action	Weight	Time	Space
THRUST	firm	sudden	direct
PRESS	firm	sustained	direct
WRING	firm	sustained	flexible
SLASH	firm	sudden	flexible
FLOAT	fine	sustained	flexible
FLICK	fine	sudden	flexible
DAB	fine	sudden	direct
GLIDE	fine	sustained	direct

CHAPTER THREE

Practice and Organization of Physical Education

Why Education in Movement?—This is a valid question since its contribution is often overlooked by both parents and education-alists. We have stated in Chapter One that the younger the child the more physical are his needs and the more necessary are opportunities for movement. A child restless for activity cannot concentrate on things of a more sedentary nature. Children delight in movement. Who, having seen a young child jump, roll, balance, push, pull, dance, throw, build and knock down, can doubt this? While the child may be unable to verbalise his emotion, who cannot read joy, anger, dejection and concentration through the nature of his movement? Who, having seen a child learning to walk, to skip, to control a ball and to ride a scooter, has not been aware of the child's determination to develop physical skill and seen the pleasure given by mastery of his body and the manipulation of external objects?

Our first and foremost aim always must be to provide enjoyable opportunities for physical activity. For this to be so, the activities selected, their range and method of presentation must meet the needs of each child. We used to hear much of posture, poise and carriage and many unnatural, boring, restricted and purposeless exercises resulted from an emphasis on these. If our physical education programme is balanced and natural, and the movement of the children unencumbered by inappropriate clothing and foot-wear, special postural or remedial activities will be unnecessary in the time-tabled lesson. All round bodily participation helps ensure fitness and vigour. A catholic programme embracing skill in all its aspects will provide for all the physical needs of the child.

The word 'skill' is one which may need clarification. Previously it has been held to indicate an ability to reproduce certain stereo-typed, narrowly conceived, standard movements. To us, skill means the ability to initiate or reproduce movements of a high level of difficulty with economy of effort. The degree of skill is always relative to the ability of the child. Skill may be of a dance-like

character or may involve objective body movement or manipulation.

The ability to move imaginatively and to devise one's own
response demands a knowledge of the possibilities of movement
contained in the challenge of the situation, whether this is imposed
by the task or the apparatus. The development of an understanding
of the analysis of movement should start at the infant stage. An
awareness by the child of some of the ways in which his body is
moving is the foundation upon which later knowledge can be built.
Through everyday use the vocabulary, an appreciation of the
language of movement, its application and its meaning will be
acquired.

Health Education, although present in all aspects of the Infant
School curriculum, is perhaps more obvious in its relation to
Movement Education. Healthy habits of changing and washing
need to be practised at all times. The time spent changing in the
lower classes of the Infant School should be regarded as an invest-
ment for teachers in future years. The ability of the child to dress
and undress gives him a greater degree of independence of adults
and should be regarded as part of his general education. On these
grounds there would certainly seem to be no reason why it should
be felt that the time spent in developing such skill should be taken
from, what is all too often, too short a movement lesson. Many
teachers of reception classes seeking to stimulate the growth of
dressing techniques display lists giving the names of children who
can tie their shoe laces. Other charts may bear ribbons, laces or
ties where the children may practise in order to develop the
necessary finger dexterity. The encouragement of children to help
one another, the use of elastic in 'lace-hole' plimsolls to form gus-
sets, the provision of individual shoe bags and the insistence upon
marked clothing and footwear all help to improve efficiency. After
the first term in school the teacher should not need to help the
children in dressing and undressing. Training the children to
arrange their clothes and shoes tidily when undressing will be
effort amply repaid. A useful practice, too, in order to save time
and interruption to the lesson, is to ensure that all the children
visit the lavatory before the commencement of the movement
education lesson.

During all physical education periods the children should either
be bare-foot or wear socks and plimsolls. Wearing socks only on

11

the feet should never be permitted. The least amount of clothing suitable for the weather conditions should be worn. The responsibility of keeping the children warm lies with the teacher. There is no virtue in a child wearing no more than vest and knickers on a cold day when pullovers or cardigans would be more appropriate. In other conditions woollies may perhaps be removed a few minutes after the lesson has begun. It is always better that the children should be too warm rather than risk their being cold. Jackets, dresses, skirts and ties should, however, always be removed.

When taking a movement lesson it is not necessary for the teacher to change but we suggest that she should be appropriately dressed and have suitable footwear. This is for safety, for mobility, for freedom of movement and to encourage class changing.

Another safety factor is a clean and splinter proof floor. This is particularly necessary when a hall in which lunch has just been served is to be used for physical activity. No unnecessary or dangerous items of furniture, such as glass-fronted cupboards, should be sited in the hall. Other items of furniture, for example, dining room tables and chairs should be economically and safely stacked.

Movement, fundamental to the life of us all, is even more vital in childhood. The bodily needs of strength, mobility, stamina and control alone give it an intrinsic worth to justify its major consideration in our scheme of education. Education of physical skills is not, however, our sole aim. Movement Education contributes to the development of the whole individual through physical activity. Physical benefits, together with the development of physical skills, are to be thought of only as concomitants. We are interested in more than the child's achievements. The process of learning at all stages and for all subjects in the Infant School is through personal experience. The educational value of our teaching lies not only in the child's fund of knowledge and skill but also through the processes leading to them.

Working at the same time as others without interfering with them in any way helps develop concentration and socialisation. To combine with others in partner or group activities, in getting out or putting away apparatus, gives opportunities for co-operation. Observing the rest of the class at work should help build a basis for assessment and an appreciation of the work of others. This will lead to greater understanding and subsequent improvement in personal interpretation and performance.

From the outset the emphasis in all our lessons must be on enjoyment and activity and not skill acquisition. This is not to say that we should not demand quality in the children's work but that skill is not to be developed over a narrow field by meaningless repetition. The work set must be appropriate to the child's ability and aptitude range. This means that it must be posed in such a way as to be capable of individual interpretation. The teacher's task is to see that each child works up to or near the maximum level of his ability. A pre-conceived idea of how children should answer a posed challenge must be avoided. We should work on the basis of what the child produces to aid quality, to suggest other areas for exploration and to encourage other forms of interpretation.

Observation by the teacher is a power which can only be developed by experience and, initially, by conscious effort. Many teachers have said that they are bewildered at the sight of forty children all doing different things; and that they cannot see what the children are doing. When once we understand that they are not all doing something different but showing an individual approach to a similar situation, movement analysis will become much easier. Ease of observation can only come with practice. To begin with, the teacher should select one aspect of movement bearing a relation to the task set, for example, body shape, or parts of the body being used, and look for this in the performance of an individual or of the class. After some weeks, or months, of practice in picking out specific aspects of the children's responses she will no longer have to search out the elements of movement. As a result of her experience they will make themselves readily apparent.

A teacher needs to be able to see much more than just a class at work, whether they are all involved and how they are moving. She needs, through her knowledge of her children, to be able to assess whether each child is working to the best level of his ability and to know whether he is developing a capacity for sustained effort. The use of space is a factor of which the teacher needs to be continually conscious. Children cramped at one end of the hall, or too many children working on a piece of large apparatus, will have their movement inhibited and the quality of movement and of discipline will deteriorate. The readiness of a class to make sensible use of the available working space is often an indication of its confidence. Safety too, one of our greatest responsibilities, will be endangered if the space available is not appropriate to the activity. Each form of physical education has dangers inherent in the activity which will be dealt with in greater detail in the appropriate chapter.

The teacher needs to note the development of co-operation and the integration within or rejection by the group of individual children. Something of the psychological needs of the child may be seen through such things as self-assertion, a need for attention or a lack of confidence.

We all need to be noticed. The recognition of effort and achievement together with the teacher's encouragement will act as a constant impetus to greater effort and satisfaction. There are many ways of doing this beside saying the words 'Well done!' or 'You have worked hard.' A look, smile or nod from across the hall, a class or individual commendation will often serve the purpose. Over-critical assessment may be misunderstood. An impatient tone of voice or a non-responsive teacher can lead to a dulling of pleasure and discouragement. At the Infant stage, children are particularly vulnerable to the tactless or indifferent teacher. Responsiveness and the positive attitude of the teacher towards the subject are all-important in helping to mould child opinion and in the maintenance of his confident, lively-minded approach. A child needs the stimulation that only the teacher can give. Through comment, guidance and praise the teacher acknowledges and shows appreciation of the child's efforts to accomplish the task set either by the teacher or himself. The recognition of achievement, help in the improvement of performance, or suggesting additional avenues of investigation may be given at individual, group or class level. At all times the teacher needs to be sensitive enough to know when to interrupt the class and the optimum time to be spent on an activity.

During a Movement Education lesson it is necessary for the teacher to be mobile. A teacher will spend much of her time at the edge of her class so that she can see all the children at work. Her position needs to be up sun or, when outdoors up wind, to be able better to observe and communicate with her class. When she wishes to speak to an individual or be seen by the children while they are working there may be advantage in mingling with the class, although care should be taken not to interfere with their activity.

14

With more informal and freer methods of approach some teachers become worried about noise and fear the deterioration of discipline. We believe that it is unreasonable to expect a class of infant children to work in complete silence. For the development of skills when working together, for safety and merely because it is unnatural and artificial to expect young children not to talk in enjoyable situations, we believe that a level of working noise should be acceptable. Just what this level is will depend on the activity and the proximity of other classes. Certainly at no time should it exceed that level at which the teacher can gain immediately the attention of all children. Discipline comes through the absorption of the child in his work. Interest comes by the presentation of activities through which he gets satisfaction. Satisfaction is based on achievement. The work should have contributed to the development of skill and understanding and to the child's growing mastery of himself, his body, or his perception.

At all times the children's work should be making a real demand upon their ability. A solid foundation of knowledge and experience needs to be laid if a child is to devise imaginatively his own ways of moving and be able to find solutions to limitations imposed by the theme or the apparatus. Nothing can be more boring to children, or so productive of work of low quality as the teacher who is always asking her class to find different ways of moving, when the children are insufficiently armed with knowledge or by experience and enlightened teaching to meet the task.

The development of the right attitude of the children towards the care of and respect for apparatus stems largely from the attitude and practices of the teacher. Children delight and will take pride in bright, cheerful, colourful apparatus. Teachers collectively, and individually, are responsible for the standards developed by the trouble they take in the storage of apparatus, the care which they insist the children should take in handling the apparatus, and the tidiness which is demanded when the children return apparatus during a lesson.

Children are entitled to expect a teacher to be efficient. This can only come through adequate planning and preparation with due attention being paid to organisation. Is the apparatus ready before the lesson begins? If not, can the children once they are changed, easily collect and distribute it? Do the children start work immediately they enter the hall and when they collect or exchange

15

apparatus during the lesson? Can the pace of the lesson be improved if certain children have a regular duty in handling the apparatus?

The planning of schemes of work and of individual lessons ensure continuity, avoids meaningless repetition and makes more certain the presentation of material appropriate to the needs of the class. Within the scheme of work opportunities should exist for the children to choose their own activity.

Opportunities for children to observe movement should play a part in every lesson. Observation is more than visual impression and should help to develop movement analysis, an understanding of quality and of relationships. To be purposeful it should always be related to the task in hand and not merely provide opportunities to watch others.

Periods of observation should be short and care must be taken not to break the flow of the lesson too often, or the children's concentration on the work in hand. A teacher must also be careful not to spend too much of the lesson in observation. Where possible, comments on the demonstrations should be drawn from the children through enlightened questioning. Any questions asked should be short, clear and specific. Not 'How is John moving?' but 'On what part of his body is John moving?' The children should then be allowed to return to further practice immediately. If the class is unable to supply an answer it is best not to waste further time but to explain. Then the teacher should let the children once again watch the point that she is trying to make in action. Another technique which may be usefully employed to widen the experience of the class is for the teacher to comment while a child or group is working. It is unnecessary for the teacher to demonstrate; she should use members of the class. Children of differing physical abilities and aptitudes may all be used for demonstration. All have something to contribute to the knowledge and appreciation of the class. Indeed, the wider the range of ability that the children can see amongst their numbers the greater should be the ensuing understanding and skill of the whole class. Children may be given the opportunity to watch two or three children at work simultaneously; or a group working on a piece of large apparatus or with a common idea; one half of the class may watch the other half or each child may watch a partner and then change over; or all may watch a single demonstration.

16

Points to note in connection with demonstrations are:

(a) that neither the same children nor the best performers are chosen each time;

(b) that all the children can see;

(c) that attention has been drawn to one or two aspects to observe;

(d) that all demonstrations are short;

(e) that where possible the comments come from the children;

(f) that the demonstration is followed by immediate opportunities for practice;

(g) that no attempt is made to teach too much from any one performance;

(h) that bad work is not shown for its own sake;

(i) that teaching is always positive. We look for good work on which to build not for weakness to eliminate.

The teacher will find that she can further assist the children while they are working by asking them questions which have their answers in movement, or by commenting on responses she sees in the class in order to make the children more aware of different solutions to the problem.

During each week approximately two and a half hours should be spent on movement education activities. The proportion of the time spent on various aspects will vary with the needs and age of the class and the time of year. Certainly every day there should be either a gymnastics, games or dance lesson. Normally, however, rather more time is spent on gymnastics periods than on each of the other aspects.

This chapter would be incomplete without some mention of the desirability for an 'adventure playground' to be part of the features of any infants school. Its contribution to the imaginative play and recreation of the younger children in particular cannot be over-estimated. It says much that some schools have acquired steam rollers, boats and carts which may be sited near fixed climbing apparatus. The need exists, too, for planks, boxes, bricks and barrels with which children can build their own apparatus arrangements for use in both imaginative play and physical activity. The whole beginnings of democracy may be seen in the playing together and through the free use and sharing of materials at the infant stage.

17

CHAPTER FOUR
Gymnastics

We teach gymnastics to aid the child to develop mastery of his body and to help him to reach his full potential in objective movement. By the presentation of material to which he can respond in a way appropriate to his level of skill, his interest and application will be heightened. Working close to his maximum level of achievement will also enable him to use his strength appropriately, help maintain his mobility and increase his capacity for physical work. Through his developing understanding of objective movement, he will be able to find new ways of using his body on the floor and on apparatus. These are discovered by individual experiment when he is given opportunities to investigate and create his own sequences of movement. Children delight in repetition and by repetition the quality of their movement is given opportunity to improve. Through independent, satisfying movement we hope that confidence and initiative will develop. Through satisfaction, and by recognition of achievement, adjustment to the group situation and co-operation with others will follow.

The teacher creates the environment and then sets situations which stimulate the child to draw on his own resources for his response. All children need to feel that their efforts are noticed, that they can produce movement of good quality and that they have something to contribute to the lesson. Having moved on the floor within the context of a movement idea, the children should then be given an opportunity to apply their knowledge to the use of apparatus. This may be either the large traditional climbing or agility apparatus, or take the form of various combinations of items of small apparatus. It needs to be emphasised that the latter should be used in a gymnastic way and does not therefore include such items as bats and balls. Normally hoops, skipping ropes, blocks or skittles, canes and individual mats will be all that are needed.

All lessons should be built around a central movement idea or theme which is investigated and exploited in different situations.

18

Anne

Through experiment with this central idea and with enlightened teaching the child becomes familiar with its content and his understanding of it is thereby improved. He is then able to re-apply his knowledge more ably in a different set of circumstances. Repetition is an essential if learning and skill are to be other than superficial. It is for this reason that the theme for a series of lessons should not be changed too often. The arrangement of apparatus also should not be changed too frequently.

Children at the infant stage are far more concerned with doing than feeling. Therefore the vast majority of themes used are directly concerned with bodily activity. What the child is doing is far more important than how he is doing it.

Efficient control of body weight is essential if children are to move safely in a variety of situations. The control of body weight forms the basis of all gymnastic activity. The broad theme of body awareness is broken down to give particular emphasis to some part of the body or some specific action or activity. Only in the last

19

SELECTION AND DEVELOPMENT OF LESSON THEMES
IN THE INFANT SCHOOL

(1) General body awareness emphasizing the different parts of the body able to take weight both in movement and when stopping

(2) General body awareness emphasizing specific body part

For example (a) Feet   to move on
              (b) Hands   to move from
              (c) Hips   to move on to
to balance
to go first
carried low
carried high
close together
far apart
simultaneously
alternately

(3) General body awareness emphasizing parts used in combination

  (a) adjacent parts
        rolling
        rocking
  (b) non-adjacent parts, for example, hands and feet, rocking

(4) Body action

  (a) curling
  (b) stretching
  (c) twisting

(5) Body shape

  (a) wide
  (b) narrow
  (c) round
  (d) twisted

(6) Use of direction

  (a) forwards
  (b) backwards
  (c) sideways
  (d) turning
  (e) upwards
  (f) downwards

year of the Infant school should themes concerned with the use of space be employed. The diagram (opposite) shows the suggested main areas from which themes for infant classes should be chosen in their appropriate order. Items from the first column are selected and may be investigated on a broad front in the ways shown. They may also be combined with one aspect in the second column and investigated in greater depth. The theme is first introduced in floor work where it may be further explored using small apparatus. It should then be applied to large climbing apparatus or combinations of small apparatus. These may be used to move either on to, off, over, under, around, along, across, above, below, or through.

The elements of Time, Weight, Space and Flow are present in all movements. These, as integral parts of themes, require greater understanding and are only used with older age groups.

We believe that any gymnastics lesson of more than 20 minutes duration should consist of two parts as indicated in the lesson plan over page. To achieve this satisfactorily depends on having the right apparatus available, good organisation by the teacher and a well-trained class.

Working on the theme 'Shape using ropes'

LESSON PLAN

	PART I	PART II	
F L O O R W O R K	FREE PRACTICE or INTRODUCTORY ACTIVITY		A P P A R A T U S
	TRAVELLING	GROUP WORK	
	WEIGHT TRANSFERENCE and BALANCE		
	JUMPING and LANDING		

The suggested plan shows the distribution of lesson time. The lesson should be divided into two equal parts. Part I consists of floor work and in Part II the theme which had been investigated in the first part is applied to apparatus.

It must be emphasised that the only virtue of a lesson plan is that it supplies a reminder of the ways in which the theme should be applied. In this way a balanced comprehensive approach is maintained and the different ways of moving are investigated.

There is no value in arranging the various sections of the first part of the lesson in a particular order. Sometimes sections may be combined or occasionally omitted altogether. As long as neither of these courses is pursued for too long a period no harm will be done. Lessons need to be planned if we are to develop skill in the management of our bodies in all the various gymnastic fields of application. The span of concentration at the infant stage is relatively short. It is necessary therefore to include more than one activity under each of the section headings. To get the maximum value from a lesson it is often better for the children to work for a short time on a relatively large number of activities than to spend too long on a very few.

LESSON PLAN PART I

FREE PRACTICE

The small apparatus to be used should be distributed before the lesson begins. To ensure that the time is used purposefully the children should leave the classroom knowing exactly what form the first part of the lesson will take. They should then be encouraged to start work directly they enter the Hall. Free practice gives the child an opportunity to develop skills of his own free choice. With a reception class this part of the lesson may well be more akin to free play except that the teacher through encouragement, recognition of achievement, guidance and control ensures that it is even more enjoyable and satisfying. The teacher's participation is vital for the optimum success of this part of the lesson.

On the whole we would advocate that small apparatus is not used too often during the Free Practice part of the gymnastics lesson. This is particularly true when taking reception classes as the return of a variety of apparatus is most time-consuming. If the children are allowed to use apparatus freely, a flitting from one piece of apparatus to another should be discouraged. Such equipment as balls should not be used, as the place for the practice and development of skills involving these is in the games lesson. No portable or fixed apparatus ought to be used in this first part of the lesson. Activities should be restricted to work done individually or with a partner. The teacher may ask the class to observe individual children or small groups at work.

Although this part of the lesson is for free practice this does not mean that the teacher should not direct attention to a specific area if she feels that this will more closely meet the needs or aptitudes of the class. When the children are left completely free it is good technique to ask children 'What are you practising?' before seeking to advise them.

This period is particularly valuable to the teacher for individual coaching and guidance. She should go freely about the class looking for opportunities to help the children improve their skill. The practice should be long enough to make some impact on their skill but not so long as to become boring.

The teacher may, on the other hand, decide to direct this part of the lesson, particularly on a cold day. Warming activities such as running, jumping, vigorously using the feet in different ways for

3

movements like hopping, skipping, galloping and slipping sideways movements may be selected.

TRAVELLING
In this section of the lesson the whole space of the room should be used. The keynote is vigorous activity. The children should be encouraged to travel freely around, across and along the floor of the hall prepared at all times to modify their pathway so as not to interfere with others in the class.

Examples of the ways in which different themes may be developed in this part of the lesson are:

(1) 'In what ways can you travel using only your feet?' (one after the other, both at the same time, to move in different directions etc.)

(2) 'How can you move over the floor using both your hands and feet?' (close together, far apart, one part of the body high, etc.)

(3) 'Find ways of moving on different parts of the body' (sometimes facing the ceiling, sometimes facing the floor and sometimes facing the wall, etc.)

(4) 'Can you travel about the room sometimes curled and sometimes stretched?'

(5) 'Show me ways of travelling in different directions' (forwards, sideways, using hands and feet, etc.)

By comment and by giving the class opportunities to watch one another the teacher will widen each child's knowledge of movement and enable him to achieve higher standards of work. Fluency as well as variety in movement should be developed by the teacher. Moving quietly is often indicative of control and by drawing the children's attention to the need to move softly may help to develop this.

Particular attention needs to be paid to good footwork in the Infant School. Walking and running, fundamental activities though they are, need constant attention if they are to improve. Young children have a tendency to be flat footed in their running and walking and it should be part of our responsibility to ensure good foot action and control. The range of the types of running shown by young children on their first entry to school is quite surprising. Their running is individual and often reflects something of their personality. Few move with control. The ability to move in different ways, in different directions and to change direction need our attention. Children must have constant reminders that to run lightly they must move on the balls of their feet and with 'give' in their ankles.

WEIGHT TRANSFERENCE AND BALANCE

As with all other sections of the lesson the purpose of this section is to give the child opportunities to develop management of his body. This is done by drawing attention to his ability to control the transfer of his weight from one part of his body to another and to balance. All children should aim for skill in balancing on different parts of their bodies and in the logical, smooth change from one position to another. Regular opportunities should be given to the children to take weight on their hands in order to develop arm and shoulder strength.

This part of the lesson is most important for its value as safety training. Skill in bringing various parts of the body down to the floor softly, smoothly and with control, together with an ability in rolling, need to be practised. When working later on large apparatus these skills can be put to good use, help avoid discomfort and on occasion accident. In fact we would advise that children should not use large apparatus until they have had some experience of these activities on the floor. Under the general heading Transference and Balance children may be asked to show:

(1) Ways of taking weight on different parts of the body and transferring it to other parts.

(2) Rolling in different ways.

(3) Taking their weight on their hands and bringing it back on to their feet softly (feet to the side, near, apart, etc.)

(4) Taking weight on different parts showing different shapes.

As a safety precaution when asked to take weight on their hands, children should be reminded that they need to raise the head to help avoid over-balancing or collapsing.

At the infant level the stress in all weight bearing activities must be placed on movement and not stillness. Artificiality will often result if the children are asked to hold positions which place no demand on them.

JUMPING AND LANDING

This type of activity is unfortunately often neglected during the Infant School lesson. Many children, although they find no

25

problem in jumping down from a height show a low level of skill in either jumping 'on the spot', over a low obstacle or jumping from a run. It has been said that the way in which a class jumps is often indicative of the quality of the physical education to which it has been exposed. Jumping comes under the overall umbrella of 'foot work' and should have its place in every gymnastics lesson. Few children seem to jump well naturally. It is a skill of a reasonably high level which can be developed only by practice. Quality of jumping is far more important than mere variety. The teacher may find it easier to maintain the children's interest by giving them a small piece of apparatus to jump over, along or around. Care must be taken to ensure that the children do not look down at whatever obstacle they are jumping over.

Both yielding landings, in which children are coached to 'give' in hips, knees and ankles, and resilient (bouncing) landings need to be practised to ensure balance of activity and width of experience. A yielding landing is one where the body gradually absorbs the energy of the jump. A resilient landing is one where the landing is followed immediately by vigorous muscular contraction to drive the body, once more, into the air. Landings may be practised from low jumps and stepping take-offs to give opportunities for skill to be developed. In the last year of the Infant School, to help direct the children's attention to specific aspects, it may assist the teacher to think of the activity as having three distinct parts. Each jump may be divided into:

(i) take-off   (ii) flight   (iii) landing

In this skill, as in all others, children are individual in their attainment and receptivity. Patience and the readiness to advance at the children's rate of progress will bring the optimum result. In this part of the lesson the children may be asked:

(1) 'Jump across your rope showing "give" in your landing.'

(2) 'Jump in a bouncing way along your rope.'

(3) 'Run and jump lifting one part of your body high' (hand, heel, chest, etc.)

(4) 'Show me ways of jumping keeping your feet together' (on the spot, moving, to change direction, etc.)

(5) 'Can you make a stretched (long, wide, twisted, etc.) shape while you are in the air?'

(6) 'In which different directions can you jump over your mat?'

26

SMALL APPARATUS

Small apparatus has a most important part to play in extending the range of the child's gymnastic experience. In the early stages of its introduction to the lesson it can help to show children how important it is to make full use of the available space. Pieces of apparatus distributed over the floor indicate clearly to the child whether the optimum use is being made of the floor space. Small apparatus may be used in both parts of the lesson to develop the theme under consideration. While moving over, across, around, along, through, between, into and out of a piece, or arrangement of pieces, of apparatus the children may continue to investigate or illustrate the aspect of movement being dealt with in the lesson.

Individual mats are useful, not merely to give purpose to an activity but also because they can often make working more comfortable. When the child is not skilled in the transfer of his body weight (or when the floor of the hall is cold) he will work far more happily if allowed to use an individual mat. When rolling practices are first introduced an individual mat should always be used.

Hoops may be used flat on the floor, perched horizontally at different heights when rested on skittles or on blocks, or held vertically by placing an individual mat—resting on the floor, through the hoop. The practice of having a partner to hold a hoop is an uneconomical use of working time and to be avoided.

Wooden blocks $12'' \times 3'' \times 3''$ having a grooved top are most useful items of equipment. They easily provide obstacles of different heights, lengths and shapes. Used in conjunction with canes and hoops, obstacles of a different nature may be presented. Laid flat on the floor they may provide for useful balance activities.

Skipping ropes when placed on the floor may give pathways of different shapes to follow, to travel beside, across or along or if placed in a circular shape may stimulate different responses.

Examples of activities using small apparatus are:

(1) 'Place your skipping rope on the ground and show me a jumping pattern going from one end to the other' (to travel along on different parts of your body; using only your hands and feet, etc.)

(2) 'Show me ways of jumping over (around) your mat.'

(3) 'Using your hoop either horizontally or vertically show me ways of going in and out or through. How many different parts of your body can go first?'

Using small apparatus during group work

LESSON PLAN PART II

In addition to being used in Part One, small apparatus also has an important part to play in Part Two of the lesson. One of its uses is to introduce the class to group work. As a first stage one half of the class is set to work, using perhaps hoops, while the other half is, perhaps, using skipping ropes. After a period of practice each half of the class leaves its apparatus and changes places. Using such simple arrangements should be effective immediately since the children will already be familiar with using the apparatus and also in returning it to its appropriate place. Very little time will therefore be lost on organisation.

> 'This half of the class collect a hoop and use all the space at this end of the hall. The other half collect ropes and place them stretched out along the ground at the other end. Let me see you using your apparatus for jumping in and out or along.'

After some coaching in the techniques of jumping and the stimulation of different types of jumps the informal changing of places takes place.

Soon, four groups may be used and by this time the changing round of the groups should be carried out with very little fuss. The teacher will need to plan carefully the collection and distribution of the apparatus. When the time comes to change groups the children should be taught to stand by the apparatus. It will be necessary to go through a stage where the children wait, point to the next group, move to it and wait again until told to start work. This may seem to be a slow process but the teacher can gradually streamline it as the children gain experience. In time, large apparatus groups may be introduced into this section of the lesson until seven or eight distinct arrangements are simultaneously in use. The number of groups at work may be gradually increased by the introduction of single arrangements of large apparatus. Alternatively half of each small apparatus group may be given responsibility for the erection of a simple large apparatus arrangement. In this way an immediate jump to eight groups is made. Additional large apparatus groups are then later substituted in place of the small apparatus still being used. A stage in development should be the conscious realisation by the children that in the group situation the apparatus is no longer for individual use but there to be shared. Many schools have not sufficient large apparatus to employ all the children simultaneously and will need to supplement permanently group activities with small apparatus arrangements. There is no reason why a great variety of interesting situations using small apparatus cannot be employed and enjoyed. Care should be taken not to just arrange small apparatus in line. A more random dispersal allows more flexible pathways to be used. This will also mean that children will not have to queue and that because the pathway is not prescribed no child will be held up by the child in front moving more slowly. All the children should be working all the time.

Instead of having defined groups a teacher may decide that the children should move freely at will between arrangements of apparatus. The success of this method depends on the ability of the teacher to ensure that the children understand the need not to overcrowd any piece of apparatus or to remain at any one arrangement too long. If the children are ready for this method of using the apparatus it is to be preferred to the more formal arrangement where the teacher stops the class at work and supervises the circulation of groups at a set time. Once the class gets to know its teacher well, the change over to a 'free' choice of apparatus by the children is not difficult to introduce.

LARGE APPARATUS

There is no doubt that a number of people will question our earlier assertion in this chapter that in an Infant school the gymnastic lesson should consist of both floor work and apparatus work in the same period. Many will maintain that the system whereby children have one period a week for large apparatus (usually erected by the caretaker) is the only safe and effective way for its use. The apparatus is also thought by some to be too heavy. To this our reply would be:

(1) If the apparatus is too heavy to be handled by the children then it should not be in an Infant school. There is today a vast assortment of both fixed and portable apparatus available which can be erected by properly trained children. Taking up the minimum space when not in use, strong in design although light in construction it is capable of being used in a great variety of ways. It will provide for different heights, widths and combinations of situations for the children to explore.

(2) Usually when the apparatus is erected by the caretaker, or the top class of the Infant or Junior school, almost invariably the same arrangement of apparatus is retained for a very long period. This reduces the variety of experience to which the children are exposed and means that the arrangements cannot be according to the needs of a particular class nor appropriate to the different themes on which all classes should be working.

(3) The safe, efficient carrying of the apparatus should be part of our training in physical education. Unless the children get this experience we are robbing them of a most valuable aspect of their work.

Having introduced reception children to group work by way of small apparatus, the more easily handled items of portable apparatus such as stools, small trestles or nesting bridges, bars, ladders, mats, stage boxes, planks and benches are gradually incorporated into the second part of the lesson. These too may be widened in their scope by being used in association with small apparatus. Occasionally, however, it may be fun for reception children to follow an older class which has left its apparatus in position for them.

Economy in the use of time to erect and dismantle apparatus may be effected in a number of ways:

(1) By having the apparatus dispersed around the room. In this way different classes may easily select their own arrangement of apparatus. Should widely different combinations of apparatus be required by different teachers then the distribution of apparatus around the hall can be modified termly by agreement of the staff.

(2) Apparatus should always be erected and used near to where it is stored.

(3) Arrangements of apparatus should be retained for at least half a term. By constantly changing apparatus, time is wasted in the fresh detailing and description of the arrangement required. The children also do not have sufficient time to investigate the apparatus in order to use it with sufficient variety and skill.

(4) If specific groups of children have specific responsibilities then they will develop familiarity in handling and placing the apparatus leading to greater efficiency. By changing group responsibility when arrangements of apparatus are modified the children can obtain a variety of experience in handling apparatus together with intensive periods of practice.

Hinged rope frame

It is realised, of course, that what we suggest with regard to the erection and dismantling of the large apparatus will not always be possible. Some compromise will often be necessary. Items of apparatus which children find difficult to handle may have to be erected prior to the commencement of the lesson. The number of these should be kept to a minimum. However, when ordering new items of apparatus the variety possible in its use and the ease with which it may be moved by young children should be borne in mind.

When an arrangement of apparatus is first introduced to children they should be allowed to investigate it being completely free of an imposed challenge, task or limitation. The teacher, as appropriate to the theme being used, may during this period pose such

above: *Hinged wall frame*

below: *Nesting bridges*

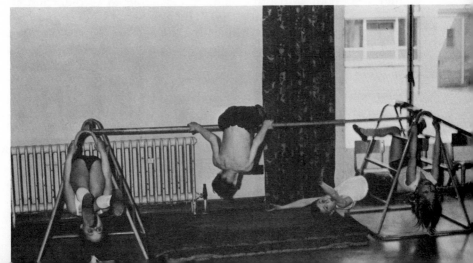

questions to individual children as 'On which part of your body are you taking your weight?' 'Which part of your body is going first?'

The teacher should constantly ask the children to seek new ways of coming from the floor on to the apparatus and ways of coming from the apparatus on to the floor. Not only for safety reasons should this be practised but the children need constant reminders that the floor is to be regarded as part of the apparatus.

After a period of practice, which will vary according to the age and experience of the class, the children may be asked to continue their investigation using the specific theme under consideration in Part One of the lesson. A teacher should always check that the apparatus has been safely erected before the children are allowed to use it. The teacher should never identify herself with a particular arrangement of apparatus but circulate among the groups giving help and advice as required. After the initial introductory stage the class should never be in groups of more than five or six children. The groups should be kept as small as possible so that all the class is working simultaneously without interfering with the work of others. By approaching apparatus from different directions and levels the children can extend the scope of their work. The variety of apparatus arrangements will stimulate variety of movement. Since the nature and combination of pieces of apparatus will present different problems within the same framework the child will have to use his intelligence and movement vocabulary to adapt his movements to it.

The teacher should see that the working noise does not rise above the necessary minimum but at the same time she should realise that it is both unrealistic and unreasonable to forbid children to discuss a joint response. The children should be encouraged to be aware of others while working. It is not anticipated that the children will be able to explore all the apparatus groups within the one lesson. The groups should be arranged so that the children have experience of a variety of activities. The teacher must ensure that the children having explored a number of pieces of apparatus during a lesson are subsequently given the opportunity to visit the remaining apparatus sections. The practice of circulating in one lesson in a clockwise direction and in the next in an anti-clockwise direction may be found to be useful. A safety precaution when changing groups is to ensure that all children have descended from the apparatus before groups are changed round.

Normally it is unnecessary for large mats to be used in association with apparatus except when jumping down may be included in the children's response. The wholesale distribution of mats cannot be recommended as an effective safety precaution. Jumping down from a height is an essential part of Movement Education in the Infant school and opportunities for such activity should be regularly presented. Such items as portable stage units are invaluable when used in such contexts.

In schools where it is necessary to have the apparatus erected before the beginning of the lesson, we would suggest that a short Part One should always be taken. The floor spaces between the apparatus may be used to revise the theme under consideration and to prepare the children before they use the apparatus. Other ways of carrying out the introductory part of the lesson are to ask the children to find different ways of travelling under the apparatus, of jumping down from different parts of the apparatus, of moving around the floor and on and off the apparatus using only the hands and feet, etc.

Some combinations of apparatus will be dismantled more quickly than others. When told to put away the large apparatus, the children should, therefore, at the same time, be given an activity which they are to practise when their task is completed.

A lesson is not complete in itself; it should be related to lessons which have taken place previously, and what is learnt in one lesson should be the foundation of subsequent lessons. In this way the child's experience of movement grows naturally, and is not the accidental result of a series of unrelated activities. What matters is not the completion of pre-planned activities. Instead, we seek to awaken, develop and cultivate the child's resources of movement in different situations. Having set a task, the teacher should see that it is accurately fulfilled, and that it helps the child to wider experience, greater clarity of response and to the highest development of his skill.

CHAPTER FIVE

Dance

'The Dance lesson is not a time for rhythmic exercises to music nor for the performance of choreographed dances but a time for creative activity'.[1] These few lines show what the attitude of the infants' teacher should be towards Dance. The Dance lesson is a time for exploration and discovery, of active participation in a widely ranging field of creative movement. Its aim is the developing control of the body as an instrument of expression and communication.

A child's delight in rhythmic movement and his dance-like response in many situations may be seen from an early age. His feelings and emotions are often seen in movement and in its accompanying facial expressions. This spontaneous, natural and often unconscious response can show the whole range of human moods. Through his body the child has a varied means of human communication. The foundations of Dance are already present. Our task is to preserve spontaneity, to enliven his response and help him to enlarge his repertoire. At the same time we should help to develop understanding, to clarify his movement and enable the child to enjoy the pleasure given by a mastery of bodily expression.

Children, of this age group, are very much concerned with action. There is tremendous absorption in activity. Children left to themselves will certainly be creative but with the help, suggestion and planning of the teacher the quality of their response will be tremendously improved. As in all Movement Education lessons, after allowing a period of free experiment, the teacher stimulates, guides and helps the child to select and clarify his movement. The teacher needs always to remember that the child learns through doing. Comment should be broad rather than detailed so as not to inhibit enjoyment or interfere with the pace of the

[1] Joan Russell, Creative Dance in the Primary School (1965), Macdonald and Evans p. 17.

lesson. To praise is to stimulate, and to criticise is to depress the infant child.

Dance should not stand in isolation. It is most easily integrated into work in other aspects of the Infant School curriculum. Music, Painting, Drama, Modelling and English can all bear a relationship to, and be enriched by association with, Dance. Because of the high level of skill required, children of this age find co-operation in objective movement activities difficult. In Dance, successful co-ordination with another child depends largely on attitude and the establishment of a relationship between the children concerned. The opportunity to develop relationship is an aspect of Dance which should enter into every lesson. By developing an awareness, and later an appreciation of the work of others, partner activities make a positive contribution. The first stage in the development of relationship is that of the child with the teacher. By her participation in the lesson the teacher encourages her class. She does not

37

work with the children but her attitude, voice and movement should reflect her understanding. Her encouragement, enjoyment and pleasure in the work of the children indicate her involvement.

As in gymnastics the lesson should have a central theme. This may vary from one lesson to the next but will normally be spread over a number of lessons in order to widen experience, to deepen understanding and to improve quality. The teacher needs to be on her guard against stressing quality of movement to the detriment of enjoyment. Another danger is the inclusion of too many activities in a lesson which allows the children insufficient time to gain experience and understanding. Opportunities for the repetition of activities must be given. To deal superficially with all the various ways of applying the theme will not fulfil the needs of the children.

Laban, in his book 'Modern Educational Dance',[1] described his sixteen basic movement themes. The first three of these together with some aspects of theme five are suitable for work at the infant stage.

Theme 1   *Body Awareness*
      (a) Movement and Stillness
      (b) Movement of specific body parts
      (c) Whole body activities

Theme 2   *Awareness of Time and Weight*
      (a) Sudden and sustained (quick and slow)
      (b) Firm and fine touch

Theme 3   *Space Awareness*
      (a) Personal and general space
      (b) Basic directions
      (c) Spatial actions

Theme 5   *Partner Work*
      (a) Alternate movement
      (b) Simultaneous movement

Leading and following, contrasting movement and matching movements when working with a partner will all be seen at the infant stage during Dance. These may be noted or used for demonstration but are too advanced to be used generally as themes.

A lesson will normally be planned in three main sections. First will come an Introductory or Warming-up period which may be

[1] Rudolph Laban, Modern Education Dance (1963), Macdonald and Evans.

Partner work

based on the material of previous lessons or be used to introduce new work. Older and more experienced children will also respond freely when a well known 'pop' record or suitable piece of gay music is used. This is followed by a section called Movement Training, which is devoted to the guided exploration of the lesson theme. The climax of the lesson draws together the work of that or previous lessons. Each lesson, although one of a series, should have its own individual aim and sense of achievement. In the Climax the children should be given an opportunity, either individually or with a partner, to show what they have learned and perhaps apply their new experience in a slightly different situation. The balance of these parts of the lesson will vary according to the age and experience of the class and the place of the lesson in the overall scheme. In order to help establish contact, to lay the foundations of future response and to draw the child's attention to the importance of listening 'Movement and Stillness' is the first theme that we recommend the teacher to use. It must be emphasised that Stillness is to be looked on as something positive and not merely as the absence of movement. It is either the position in which movement has logically ended or one from which it is about to begin. Movement is suspended rather than just stopped. The theme of Movement and Stillness may be applied to work 'on the spot', travelling, moving on the feet, moving in other ways, stopping suddenly, gradually, while coming together, and while spreading out. These, as well as training in the need to listen, will afford plenty of material for the early lessons.

Continuing with the major theme of Body Awareness, we then consider the use of specific body parts. First we concentrate on the feet; these may be used to move on, with large steps, small steps, continuously, suddenly, lightly, strongly, on different parts, moving forwards, backwards, sideways, turning, jumping, striding, lifting the feet high, keeping them close to the floor, moving quickly, slowly, with accompaniment and without accompaniment. The next group of lessons should be concerned with the use of the hands—where they can reach, how they can dance to the music, if they can show strength, move strongly or gently, push, pull, shake, move together or apart, singly or simultaneously, open out, close up, gently touch each other, the floor, or other parts of the body, clap or lead off into a dance. Next, the teacher will deal with use of the hands and feet together. She can then move on to consider the use of other parts of the body in a similar way. The use of the elbows, shoulders, head and knees, to lead a movement, to meet the floor and each other; to move independently or together until finally the child is ready for more advanced considerations.

Having given experience of the action of individual body parts, the teacher may now concentrate on whole body action while travelling, leaping and turning. Continuing with the theme of body awareness, emphasis can now be shifted to the consideration of shape. From moving into and from stretched, curled and twisted positions the children will be encouraged to move showing the positive actions of opening, closing and twisting. Opportunities to feel the nature of spiky, rounded, symmetrical, asymmetrical movements while rising, falling, advancing and retreating should be given. Whole body participation in stepping and jumping as well as in locomotion needs to be experienced.

In Dance, since we do not have the additional discipline of function to consider, children are able to concentrate more easily on movement. Through creative movement we can develop understanding more easily without having the restriction of an

Spiky dance

objective result. For this reason even at the Infant School stage in Dance we can consider the elements of movement. The second major theme will develop the awareness of weight and time. Strong and gentle movements, exemplifying the firm and fine touch of the weight element, may be experienced and appreciated. Children should be exposed to this experience in elementary, broad situations. Time should not be spent on fine, precise movements requiring great concentration. The children are then taken through experiences concentrating on the element of time. Sudden movement is more easily appreciated than sustained movement, and the approach to both is often best through a first consideration of quick and slow movement.

Each of these aspects of movement is dealt with in the context of the first theme. First consideration is given to their impact on individual parts of the body, for example, the feet and elbows. They are then applied to whole body action as has been described earlier in this chapter. Successive contrasts of movement may be stimulated by the playing either of different percussion instruments or the same instrument played in different ways.

The children are then led to a consideration of the use of space. This may start by developing awareness, through exploration, of personal space. Movement away from, towards and around the body centre and of the spatial areas in front, behind, above, below and to the side; the drawing of shapes, such as circles and figures of eight with different parts of the body, together with the incorporation of these aspects of movement already experienced, may be imposed. The children should then investigate the straight, curving and twisting pathways which they may trace in general space. There should be a growing awareness of others in the class, not merely as obstacles to be avoided or given room in which to move, but as having a particular relationship with one another as well as with the teacher.

Without doubt, percussion is the fundamental and most important stimulus in Infant Dance. From the earliest lessons the teacher will use her voice or percussion instruments to stimulate the response of her class. Since the latter give rhythm and timbre rather than melody, percussion instruments are able to give a simple but varied sound stimulus. Classical records, which are occasionally used for dance in the Infant School, are not suitable and teachers are advised not to use them. To begin with, percussion may be used almost as an accompaniment to the movement of the children. Gradually the realisation of the difference between moving to such varying instruments as a shaken tambourine, a beaten tambour, bells and cymbals will become established. Children will need opportunities to listen to and talk about the differing sound qualities of the various items of percussion. Through experience, the children are encouraged to decide what are the appropriate movements to sudden, continuous, loud, soft and rhythmical use of a wide range of instruments. Although content and variety of experience are more important than a narrow emphasis on quality, as the children grow so too may their responsibilities be widened and more be demanded from them. They are taught not only to suit their movement to the stimulus, but also to appreciate that stillness has its own contribution to make.

The following instruments are useful: tambour, tambourine, gong, drum, cymbals, bells, triangles, skulls, castanets, maracas and chime bars. Children can also be encouraged to make their own improvised instruments based on those which they can shake, beat or use to produce sound in other ways. Gradually the understanding grows whereby the children are able to dance according to the quality of movements suggested by the instrument. Variations, too, of tempo, strength and rhythm will all elicit different responses. The range of experiences open to the class of a discerning teacher is extremely wide.

Later, the children should be able to select and play instruments of their own choice. Having experimented with the sound possibilities of the instrument the child should then be given opportunities to dance and to acompany himself and others. In this way the children are subjected to the additional discipline, not only of moving suitably to the sound which the instrument can produce, but also of playing appropriately to fit their particular dance. This represents quite an advanced stage and, before being able to do this, much work will need to be done. One child may play the instrument while his partner dances. Children may share or have individual instruments or one child may play for a group of children. It takes some time for the level of skill to develop when children can play certain instruments well while dancing themselves. When first attempting this, it is necessary for the child to have an instrument which spontaneously produces sound as he moves. For this reason bells are more suitable than instruments

43

Dancing with percussion

such as tambours or blocks which require co-ordination of hand and eye. If the children are to be given wide ranging opportunities, this aspect of teaching will cover a large number of lessons. In the last year of the Infant School partner responses of a high level of quality and understanding may often be developed.

Percussion instruments may be used also in connection with drama which should supplement the work in Movement Education in the Infant School. The body, too, may be used to make a whole variety of percussive sounds. Finger snapping, hand clapping, body slapping may all help to accentuate a movement.

As the confidence and experience of the class grow if environmental conditions are suitable, the children can be encouraged to use vocal sounds both to accompany and act as a stimulus to their movement. At the infant stage these will be of short duration and tend to be repetitive. It is realised that this could be fraught with difficulty for the inexperienced teacher and should only be

Piercing

attempted when she is confident that her class is ready for it. Quite often it will arise spontaneously from the class and in this case it is to be encouraged rather than inhibited. The teacher must, of course, ensure that some children do not attempt to take advantage of the new permissiveness.

Action words, too, can be used in the Infant School both to widen the vocabulary of the class and to act as a stimulus to dance. Words to be used may come from the daily story, from poetry (some poems abound in suitable words) or from the children themselves. After working on individual words, older children may choose their own short sequence of three words and develop their own response to illustrate them in action. The words from a poem should not be read while the children are moving. The teacher might like to consider the words in terms of particular actions and, in selecting a sequence for the children, choose words from different groups. Other words based on spatial awareness or the quality of movement they suggest may be considered.

EXAMPLES OF WORDS TO STIMULATE MOVEMENT

LOCOMOTION	creeping, dashing, swooping, weaving
JUMPING	leaping, springing, bounding, hopping
TURNING	twisting, twirling, winding, screwing
STILLNESS	freezing, balancing, holding, pausing
GESTURE	rising, drooping, swelling, lifting
SPATIAL AWARENESS	surrounding, piercing, circling, cutting
MOVEMENT QUALITY	heavily, lightly, strongly, daintily

The recommendation that the teacher should not read to the children while they are moving applies, too, to the use of stories for dramatic experience. There is a common belief that a presentation of a lesson with a dramatic basis provides little difficulty. It is, in fact, a teaching technique which requires a great deal of preparation and planning and a deep knowledge of movement if it is to be really successful. Rather than present a traditional story acted out by the children, which becomes little more than a superficial dramatic representation, the essential movement situations contained in it should be extracted and experienced by the whole class. In this way the richness of the experience to which they are exposed makes the time spent worth while. At a later stage the various parts of the story may be brought together, and an individual child or groups of children given specific parts for the story to be told in movement. This should be of short duration and may then be repeated with the children changing the parts which they have played. This type of activity exists in its own right and is not suitable for presentation. If this happens it becomes over-rehearsed, spontaneity is lost and, almost invariably, the children who need to benefit most, suffer by comparison with their fellows. The stimulus given by the story is more important than its fulfilment as a completed whole.

Seasonal activites such as Bonfire night, or Circuses, may provide ideas around which to weave a series of lessons. Such things of common interest, such as Cowboys and Indians or inter-planetary travel, may also be used. It is easy to understand how the children can be involved in such lessons and how the material can flow into and from their work in English and other creative activities. It must be stressed that dramatic stimulus should not be used until the children are confident in a good movement vocabulary.

As previously stated we do not recommend the use of recorded classical music as a stimulus for Infant Dance. The music is too complicated to serve any real purpose. Small children cannot dance to long pieces of music and any music selected should be short and simple in structure. A number of special sets of records have been made to provide suitable stimulus for Infant Dance. Unfortunately, 'bands' on some of these records are rather short and difficult to find easily. It is a useful practice to record a sequence from such records several times on tape both to enable the teacher to repeat the sequence and also by using the revolution counter to find the part required more quickly.

Finally, mention should be made of the B.B.C. Music and Movement programme. Quite obviously it is better for the teacher to be able to devise, present and develop material suitable to the needs of her own class. It is, however, realised that many teachers need, at the moment, to rely on B.B.C. programmes. We should like to recommend that these lessons, when taken, should not stand in isolation. They should always provide the basis for a subsequent lesson. The lessons now may be made relevant to the needs of the class. The teacher may extract body actions or the aspects of movement under consideration and help improve the quality of the children's response. Help may also be given to enable them to move in the situations used with greater variety and individuality.

Moving stealthily

The pamphlets which are published by the B.B.C. in connection with these programmes have been carefully prepared to help teachers. By studying them the teacher can ensure that she is familiar with the movement aspects to be covered in the programme.

Dance is probably one of the most neglected parts of Infant Education today. Its teaching can be one of the most rewarding aspects of the curriculum. It is hoped that this chapter provides sufficient material for a start to be made and shows how this may be developed to the point where the teacher is ready for more advanced study.

48

CHAPTER SIX

Games

We cannot emphasise too strongly the recommendation that teachers do not mix the material of the three basic types of lessons covered in this book. To practise such skills as throwing, catching and hitting in the same lesson as expressive movement can only lead to confusion and inefficiency. Gymnastics and Dance will be taken largely in the environment of the school hall. The quality of surface necessary for the development of games skills is less critical than that required for Gymnastics. The games lesson, too, will often need greater space than is available in the school hall. This is necessary for safety reasons and to provide adequate opportunities to fully investigate, and practise with, the equipment. Sufficient space is vital if the children are to learn to control and to move with the apparatus. The fact that lessons involving the use of small apparatus are more vigorous enables such lessons to be conducted outside when it would be most inappropriate to take a gymnastics lesson. There is, however, a place for lessons involving practice with small apparatus taking place in the school hall. This is particularly true with reception classes, but the need for more space will grow apparent as the children become older and more skilled. In some school halls, skipping with any age group would be an inappropriate class activity and the teacher should always be conscious of the dangers involved in the use of some items of equipment—in particular, bats.

Lessons involving the manipulation of small apparatus, are, for the sake of simplicity, covered by the omnibus term Games. This title must not be taken to imply that team games are advocated in the Infant School. Time spent on such activities is time wasted. A games lesson, at this stage, is one structured to expose the children to opportunities to experiment with, and develop skill in, the control of a wide range of easily handled equipment.

If we are to introduce children to an extensive range of skills then a plentiful supply of a variety of apparatus is essential. A wide choice, even within a specific type of apparatus, with differences of size, weight, shape, texture and resilience is desirable. Balls, ranging from football to golf ball size, rugby balls, inflated, sorbo, plastic and rubber balls should all be available. Bats of different shapes, but always of a size to be handled easily by infant children, should be used. Half-length broom handles will provide for a different skill and call for more precision in use to control apparatus. Hoops of different materials, wood, cane and plastic of varying sizes 18, 24, 30 and 36 inches in diameter will serve to widen experience.

Some items will need to be available in sufficient numbers to equip each child in the largest class in the school. On the other hand, only half this number will be required for some items, and for others only very few pieces will be needed.

We believe that a central pool of equipment, kept in properly constructed storage containers, which is available to each class in the school, is to be much preferred to the practice of allowing each class its own equipment. The latter is wasteful and represents an inefficient use of available expenditure.

Assuming the largest class in the school consists of 40 children, we recommend that equipment should be available on the following scale.

40	$2\frac{1}{2}''$ sorbo balls
40	$2\frac{1}{2}''$ airflow balls
40	skipping ropes
40	bean bags
40	hoops
20	play bats
20	$2'$ sticks
20	canes
20	$12'' \times 3'' \times 3''$ blocks
10	$7''$ balls
10	$4''$ balls
10	plastic shuttlecocks
8	tenni-quoits
4	size 3 rugby balls
4	$5''$ rubber ferruled poles
3	pairs adjustable stilts
	Box playground block chalk

It will, of course, be necessary to have additional items in store to supplement stocks in case of loss or breakage.

The practice of having a special box or wastepaper basket for each type of equipment is not to be recommended. It is preferable to have easily portable, compartmentalised baskets of light construction which can carry a variety of small apparatus. These can then be collected by the children at the commencement of the lesson and transported from the store room to the playground or field. By distributing the baskets around the edge of the teaching area the collection and return of the apparatus is facilitated. The lesson will thus gain in efficiency and there will be no tendency for a break-down in discipline to occur through overcrowding.

An added recommendation is that the equipment should be colour coded. Red bean bags, red balls, red tennis-quoits and red tagged skipping ropes should be stored in a red basket. Each group can then identify its own equipment and will take a pride in it. This method also allows for quickly checking that all apparatus has been returned at the conclusion of an activity.

The fact that the term 'Games' is used (after all, Manipulative Skills would be a rather unwieldy title) must not lead teachers to think of the equipment being used only in the same skill context as is found in the Major Games. First, such things as hoops and skipping ropes would have no place in such a scheme. Secondly, the function of the lesson is to widen the children's experience of the nature and possibilities of the equipment and not the development of specific skills. The children need to discover the ways in which the equipment may be appropriately used. Occasionally, when freedom to develop new and personal ways of using small apparatus is given the children will use it inappropriately and in an illogical way. This is to be expected, periods of investigation and exploration will often need the teacher's guidance and help. To begin with the children will be given opportunities to use only one piece of apparatus at a time. At a later stage the combination in the use of similar and dissimilar pieces of apparatus will be investigated.

The Lesson Plan which we advocate at 'reception' level is simply:

(1) Introductory Activity or Free Practice

(2) Skill Development

(3) Final Activity

51

Later the last section is changed so that various skills are practised in small groups. The Lesson Plan then becomes:

(1) Introductory Activity or Free Practice

(2) Skill Development

(3) Group Work

As with gymnastics, the manner in which Part I of the lesson is used depends on the appreciation of the situation by the teacher. The younger the class, the greater is the need for a longer period of experiment, of individual coaching, stimulation and encouragement by the teacher. On a colder day the teacher may eliminate Free Practice completely and direct the work more specifically to ensure that no child is cold. Vigorous running, hopping, striding and jumping activities should be used. If Free Practice is decided upon, the teacher may either allow the children to be completely free in their selection of apparatus or indicate the type to be used. In the latter case the child is still 'free' since no particular skill has been selected. For example, if balls are to be used, he is free to practise such activities as throwing and catching (individually, with a partner, against a wall), bouncing, dribbling, aiming or kicking. The teacher, on occasion, will find the need to guide the selection of the apparatus by the children. Some boys when allowed a free choice may always choose a large ball, some girls a skipping rope. If this was allowed to continue it could lead to a narrowing of their exposure to skill development. The selection of activities by the children of those things at which they are quite good performers, or at which they are not very good, are other ways of varying the challenge given in this part of the lesson.

When children have been given a free choice they should work on the piece of apparatus they have selected for a reasonable time and not be allowed to continually change it. In this, as in all else, the teacher has to be aware of individual differences and recognise that the span of concentration of each child varies. She has to be flexible in handling such situations. Practice must be long enough to be worth while but not so long as to allow the children to become bored. During periods of Free Practice the teacher, before offering her help, is advised always to ask 'What are you practising?' 'What are you trying to make your apparatus do?'

Recognition by the teacher, her praise and guidance are vital factors. The teacher must be careful not to become detached from either her class or any individuals in it. This is a period for individual coaching and the teacher needs to circulate among the class.

The children's practices may evolve into a specific type of skill having a direct relationship to a traditional games response. Recognisable skills will emerge and the teacher should aid in the development of these as with all others. Attention paid to the basic techniques such as eye on the ball, appropriate use of strength, relaxation, the way to hold equipment for its most effective use will all help to develop the awareness of the children. Through breadth of personal experience, the children are led to find the most economical and effective ways of control.

As in all other aspects of infant education, development by exploration through selection and clarification to re-application and extension is followed. The experimental stage gives opportunity to become familiar with the particular properties of a piece of apparatus. Initially, this is invariably carried out by the hands or feet. Even when such skills as hitting are first used the hand rather than the bat is the implement to be employed. The children discover ways in which to use the apparatus 'on the spot', while moving, against a wall, whether it is easily stopped, what other parts of the body may be used to control it, which other activities may be practised while using the equipment, and what other items can be used in combination with it.

The teacher must ensure that the skill is appropriate to the piece of apparatus being used, that it is not dangerous and that it will not cause damage. Sticks are not made for throwing or bean bags for hitting. Wildly chasing after equipment or not keeping a firm grip on such things as bats is to be firmly discouraged. Teachers need also to be able to observe whether contact with the apparatus is sensitive and effective; whether the whole body is playing its part or whether action is isolated. Are the children developing in confidence? Are they able to continue the practice of the skill for longer periods? Can they use the apparatus moving at different speeds, in different directions, using different degrees of strength? Does their level of skill enable them to combine with another child in its practice? Are they, in fact, developing a mastery of the apparatus with which they are practising?

All the children will be at different stages of development, some will be inhibited, some over-vigorous and some unco-ordinated while others are ready to work with a partner. The teacher has to be constantly aware of the abilities of all the children in her class and the need for individual, group or class coaching. All that has been said about the use of demonstration on page 17 applies equally well to this type of lesson.

When children are working freely in a playground or on a field it is often necessary to define the areas in which the children may operate. Markings, a line of skittles or other equipment, or a clearly defined feature may be used to delineate where the children may work. Playground markings, too, need to be simple and should not be overcrowded. Where it may be necessary for markings to overlap it is often useful to use paints of two different colours. White and yellow is a popular combination. Two lines 60 feet long and 30 feet apart, a number of circles fourteen feet or sixteen feet in diameter and some rectangular areas 8 feet by 12 feet divided lengthways and across should suffice for most purposes. A horizontal line and targets of different sizes at various levels are useful additional markings where suitable blank walls are available.

Despite popular opinion more accidents take place in the playground, than in the hall when children are using large apparatus. Good safety practices during the games lesson are vital. When attention is focussed on apparatus, the children will need constant reminders about the dangers of collision. Children should never run to or turn on a wall, but rather cross or turn at a line. Racing activities should take place across or up, and never down, a slope. The need for appropriate footwear and clothing cannot be overemphasised.

All teachers, although allowing the children to create and select activities, should be aware of the tremendous range of skills possible. When the need for more direct teaching arises the teacher may then draw from the ideas given below as are appropriate to her own class.

Suitable activities to include in the lesson may be classified first as those not involving the manipulation of apparatus but having their place in the games lesson.

54

ACTIVITIES WITHOUT APPARATUS

Walking
Running
Striding
Hopping
Skipping

- different directions
- different pathways
- different speeds
- small steps, big steps
- stopping suddenly
- self competition
- in, out and over apparatus

Jumping and Landing

- on the spot
- over and round apparatus
- moving with jumping
- from a run
- for height
- from a height
- for length
- turning
- in different directions
- off one foot
- off two feet

ACTIVITIES WITH APPARATUS

Most of the activities listed below may be varied by taking place on the spot or while moving, while moving in different directions, on different pathways, with different speeds, using one hand (foot), using the other hand (foot), using one hand (foot) alternately, using both hands and with a partner. Some of the undermentioned activities should not be carried out in the confines of the school hall.

Skipping

- building a pattern
- forwards
- backwards
- turning
- self competition
- at a deep level
- in a group

Activities with hoops $\begin{cases} \text{skipping} \\ \text{bowling} \\ \text{rotating on parts of body} \\ \text{spinning (around, to return)} \\ \text{to jump over} \\ \text{to pass through while moving} \\ \text{one hoop between two} \\ \text{one hoop each} \end{cases}$

Small and Large Balls

Bouncing
Catching
Throwing over arm
       under arm

Hitting hand
     play bat
     stick

Aiming
Rolling

Dribbling with foot
     with hand
     with stick

$\begin{cases} \text{for distance} \\ \text{for height} \\ \text{for accuracy} \\ \text{for continuity} \\ \text{using wall} \\ \text{with bouncing} \\ \text{without bouncing} \\ \text{using different parts of the body} \end{cases}$

Kicking
Passing with hand
     with foot

Dropping catch

Quoits $\begin{cases} \text{throwing} \\ \text{bowling} \\ \text{spinning} \\ \text{catching in different ways} \end{cases}$

With a partner $\begin{cases} \text{one piece of apparatus between two} \\ \text{one piece of apparatus each} \end{cases}$

Bean bags are useful pieces of apparatus for throwing and catching activities at the reception stage because they do not roll or need to be chased when missed, and because they wrap themselves around the hand of a child they are easily caught.

For many activities at the top end of the infant school pseudo-games situations may be contrived by using a line as a net for hand tennis or for knocking a shuttlecock or ball across; a net may be constructed by using skittles and canes; a goal or wicket may be marked on a wall. While such arrangements are not essential they often help the child in some of his efforts towards adult identification. This is a characteristic part of children's life at this stage. Although this aspect will not need major consideration, it may stimulate interest and application to occasionally recognise it.

In Part 3 of the lesson after the reception stage, skills are practised in group situations. On no account should this involve competition with another child. The emphasis should be on playing at the same time or playing with and not against other children. It is to be looked upon as an opportunity for the further building of skill in a different situation and in co-operation with others. The work will normally be related to the particular activities of the lesson although it may also serve to revise skills previously introduced. Practices may be either individual or involve a partner. The children move round from group to group in a similar informal way to that described in Chapter 4. From working with only two groups at the reception stage the number may be gradually increased up to as many as eight groups, in the last year, all working on different tasks. The nature of the activities will depend on the weather. Good organisation and planning are vital if the children are to derive maximum benefit.

APPENDIX

Lesson Plans

Below are given typical lessons prepared in the way required of students at Brentwood College of Education while on School Practice.

GYMNASTICS (1)

Class: Reception. Since reception classes may be at very different stages of development the teaching material given below represents a selection of activities which may be taken when working on this theme.

Theme: Body awareness—feet.

Apparatus: Hoops, large apparatus.

ACTIVITY	LIMITATION	TEACHING POINTS
Opening activity	Run about the room, using all the space, stopping on signal.	Ensure good use of space. Run softly on balls of feet. Practise stopping suddenly.
Travelling	(1) Show different ways of moving on your feet.	Using one foot, alternate or simultaneous use of feet.
	(2) Show how you can move on different parts of your feet.	Heels, balls of the feet, outsides of the feet.
	(3) Move with your feet sometimes close together, sometimes far apart.	Use demonstration to show variety of response.
Weight transference and balance	(1) Place your hands on the floor and jump your feet into the air.	Keep your head back. Bring your feet down softly. Take off and land sometimes on one foot sometimes on two.
	(2) Lie on your back. Find out how many different places you can reach with your feet.	Stretch your feet away from you. Can they sometimes be in the air and sometimes touching the floor?
Jumping and landing	(1) Collect a hoop. Jump in and out and around your hoop.	Light, bouncing landings. Sometimes use one foot, sometimes two feet.
	(2) Jump over your hoop.	'Give' in knees, hips and ankles on landing. Try to jump really high.
Group work	Find ways of moving on to, along and from the apparatus.	Approach apparatus from different directions. Do not queue.
Final activity	Put away apparatus, find a space, place hands on the floor and show how high you can jump your feet into the air.	

58

GROUP WORK (1)

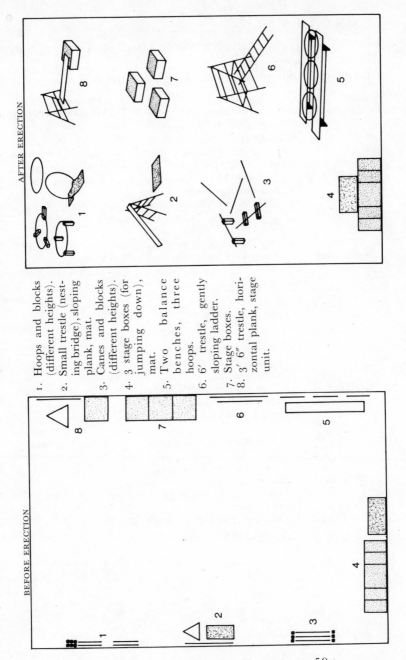

BEFORE ERECTION

AFTER ERECTION

1. Hoops and blocks (different heights).
2. Small trestle (nesting bridge), sloping plank, mat.
3. Canes and blocks (different heights).
4. 3 stage boxes (for jumping down), mat.
5. Two balance benches, three hoops.
6. 6' trestle, gently sloping ladder.
7. Stage boxes.
8. 3' 6" trestle, horizontal plank, stage unit.

59

GYMNASTICS (2)

Class: Top Infants. Number in class: 40. Time: 25 minutes.
Theme: Twisting.
Apparatus: Individual mats. Large apparatus.

ACTIVITY	LIMITATION	TEACHING POINTS
Free practice	Collect an individual mat. Show me ways of moving over, around and across it.	Individual encouragement and coaching.
Weight transference and balance	(1) Put your hands on your mat, jump your feet off the ground to bring them down in a different place.	How far can you make your feet move to the side?
	(2) Balance on different parts of your body. Twist until you come down into another balancing position.	Are you really twisting as you move?
Jumping and landing	(1) Jump over your mat and turn to face another direction.	Soft landing. Can you take off from either and both feet? Can you show more twist in the air? Can you turn to the right and to the left?
	(2) Jump towards your mat and continue your turn as you move over it.	Try to show continuity.
Travelling	(1) Show ways of travelling on your hands and feet, or flat to the floor twisting as you move.	Try to show continuity.
	(2) Show ways of travelling on all sorts of body parts twisting as you travel.	Try to show continuity.
Group work	Show ways of twisting to arrive on, to travel over and to leave the apparatus.	
Final activity	Show balancing positions in which you are really twisted.	

60

GROUP WORK (2)

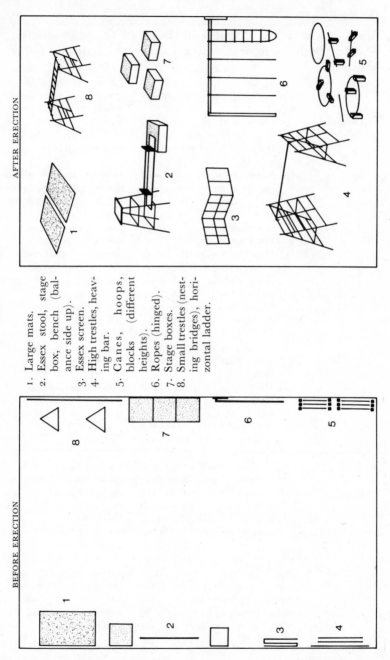

BEFORE ERECTION

AFTER ERECTION

1. Large mats.
2. Essex stool, stage box, bench (balance side up).
3. Essex screen.
4. High trestles, heaving bar.
5. Canes, hoops, blocks (different heights).
6. Ropes (hinged).
7. Stage boxes.
8. Small trestles (nesting bridges), horizontal ladder.

61

DANCE (1)

Age: 5–6 years. Number in class: Time: 25 minutes.
Theme: Body awareness, with emphasis on hands and feet.

ACTIVITY	LIMITATION	TEACHING POINTS
Introductory	Usuing all the space, dance all over the floor stopping at signal.	Encourage sensible use of space and immediate stillness at the signal.
Movement Training	(1) Dance with feet far away from the ground.	Knees to be lifted in the air.
	(2) Dance with feet near to the ground.	Footwork to be soft and light.
	(3) Move about the floor with big steps going down into the ground.	Steps to be strong, but *not* heavy. Encourage children to slowly press feet down into the floor.
	(4) Move about the floor with small steps.	Light, quick, sudden movements of the feet.
	(5) Dance all over the space using sometimes big slow steps, and sometimes small quick steps.	Make sure that the children work without getting too near one another.
	(6) Make your feet dance on the spot.	Use of different parts of the feet—heels, toes, etc.
	(7) Make your hands dance in the air, sometimes near to your body, sometimes far away.	Use of levels and directions; high, low, in front, behind, to the side, etc.
	(8) Hide your hands; make them dance out slowly, then hide away quickly.	Use all your fingers, trying to make them move very quickly, or very slowly.
	(9) Now make them dance out quickly, and hide away slowly.	
	(10) Curl up small, with hands hidden; let your hands lead you high up into the air, and then make your hands and feet dance. At signal curl up quickly.	Curl up tightly, hands slowly move upwards, dancing very lightly. When hands are high in the air, the feet dance on the spot.
Climax	Develop solo dance; start curled up, with hands hidden, hands gradually lead you up high, then dance all over the floor, sometimes with big or little steps, sometimes with feet far away from or near to the ground. At signal, slowly curl	Children can be asked to respond to stimulus of percussion instrument played by the teacher, or they can dance freely to their own rhythm, merely responding to final signal.

DANCE (2)

Age: Top Infants.
Theme: Developing awareness of body shape.
Percussion: Tambourine, Maracas and other percussion instruments for use by the children.

ACTIVITY	LIMITATION	TEACHING POINTS
Introductory Activity	(1) Standing, shake your hands in as many places as you can.	Continuous light shaking. Use space in front, behind, high, low and to both sides.
	(2) Repeat, on signal stop and hold position you are in.	Sudden stop. Awareness of shape.
Movement Training	(1) Dance freely about room showing the same light continuous movement.	Let the hands lead the movement sometimes high sometimes near the floor.
	(2) As above, on signal stop showing a strongly held position.	Is the shape you are making firm and clear?
	(3) Curl up on floor, rise with spikey movements; on signal sink softly back on to floor.	Use of fingers, elbows, knees, feet, to show spikeyness. Smooth transfer of weight to the ground.
	(4) From position on floor rise with a rounded movement and return with spikey movements.	Emphasise smooth growth of movement.
	(5) Freely mix ways of growing and returning.	Children to provide own vocal accompaniment where appropriate.
	(6) Make up a spikey dance.	Emphasise sudden changes of shape.
	(7) Show smooth changes of shape as you dance.	
Climax	With a partner make up and accompany a dance using percussion and/or voice. One or both may dance. The dance starts near the ground, grows and then moves using both spikey and smooth movements.	Free choice of percussion instruments. Clear beginning, middle and end. Circulate freely encouraging and helping individual couples.

GAMES (1)

Class: Reception. Time: 25 minutes.

Aim: To encourage a quick response to the teacher and to introduce the children to some of the skills involved in the control of small balls.

Apparatus: Small balls—one for each child.

ACTIVITY	LIMITATION	TEACHING POINTS
Opening activity	(1) Running freely stopping on signal.	Look for open spaces.
	(2) Striding freely about the playground.	Move on balls of the feet.
	(3) Running and jumping over a line when you come to it.	'Give' in ankles, knees and hips.
	(4) Choose any item of small apparatus and practise freely with it.	Individual help and coaching.
Skill training	(1) Put away your apparatus, collect a ball, and play with it freely.	Apparatus to be put away neatly.
	(2) Show ways of controlling the ball using your hands.	Keep your eye on the ball. Make good use of space.
	(3) Show ways of controlling the ball using your feet.	Keep the ball close. Push it forwards using the sides of the feet.
	(4) Show ways of bouncing your ball.	Continuous pat bouncing: then as strongly as you can.
	(5) Roll your ball, run after it and stop it in different ways.	
Final activity	Let me see you hopping. Can you hop on either foot? Count the number of hops you take between the two lines. Can you make bigger hops? Count them.	Use of arms and 'other' leg.

GAMES (2)

Class: 2nd year.   Time: 25 minutes.
Aim: To give practice in throwing and catching.
Apparatus: Small balls, large balls, tennis quoits, skipping ropes.

ACTIVITY	LIMITATION	TEACHING POINTS
Opening activity	Free practice with any piece of small apparatus.	Individual coaching, encouraging a wide variety of activities.
Skill training	(1) Using small balls show patterns of bouncing.	Soft, relaxed wrist. High bounces and low bounces.
	(a) standing still	
	(b) while moving	
	(2) Practise throwing and catching.	Keep your eye on the ball. Form a cup with your hand to receive the ball.
	(a) standing still	
	(b) while moving	
	(3) Drop the ball and try to catch it before it touches the ground.	Watch the ball carefully. Relaxed arm.
	(4) Practise throwing and catching with a partner.	Do not get too far away from your partner. Pass underhand.
	(a) standing still	
	(b) while moving	Can you sometimes catch a ball after it has bounced?
Group work	Four groups working in pairs.	Circulate, helping as required.
	(1) Throwing, catching, rolling and fielding a tenniquoit.	
	(2) Passing a large ball using hands or feet.	
	(3) Aiming, throwing, rolling, catching or fielding a small ball using a skittle as a target.	
	(4) Skipping.	Consolidation of previously practised skill.